Beyond the Jewels and Grandeur

THE HOUSES ON NORTH GREEN STREET, GAINESVILLE, GEORGIA

HELEN M. MARTIN

AuthorHouse™
1663 Liberty Drive
Bloomington, IN 47403
www.authorhouse.com
Phone: 1 (833) 262-8899

Because of the dynamic nature of the Internet, any web addresses or links contained in this book may have changed since publication and may no longer be valid. The views expressed in this work are solely those of the author and do not necessarily reflect the views of the publisher, and the publisher hereby disclaims any responsibility for them.

Any people depicted in stock imagery provided by Getty Images are models, and such images are being used for illustrative purposes only. Certain stock imagery © Getty Images.

This book is printed on acid-free paper.

ISBN: 978-1-6655-0173-6 (sc)
ISBN: 978-1-6655-0174-3 (hc)
ISBN: 978-1-6655-0172-9 (e)

Library of Congress Control Number: 2020918929

Print information available on the last page.

Published by AuthorHouse 05/13/2021

author HOUSE

Beyond the Jewels and Grandeur

Helen M. Martin

In memory of Marian Collier Martin Hosch, a dear cousin and friend, and in appreciation of Heyward C. Hosch, Jr., whose grandfather built the Hosch House on Green Street in 1907. Today, it remains the only house with the original family still occupying it.

Marian Collier Martin Hosch

September 6,1931–February 10, 2020

Contents

Gainesville, Georgia   North Green Street

Gainesville, Georgia ca. 1907

This is a post card of North Green Street looking north, where Academy Street intersects Green Street from the right. The street trolley is visible returning from Gower Springs. This post card was printed in Germany by Robertson and Law. It has a 1910 postmark from Atlanta to Thomasville, Georgia

If one wonders where Green Street got its name, it was named after Dr. R. E. Green who was the owner of the street trolley that ran down Green Street. He also had a beautiful home to the right of where the post office is located today.

PREFACE

This author is certainly not an expert on architectural concepts, but enjoys an art history background and love for art. Many hours were spent walking and observing all of the changes that were taking place on North Green Street. It is hoped that as one reads about the history and architectural features of the remaining houses, there will be a renewed appreciation for those who worked to keep them from the wrecking-ball crew. The book pages describe features of the varied architectural styles and types of houses constructed from the late 1800s to the 1939 time period.

The purpose of the book is to provide an easy to read and understanding of the versatile architectural designs in the world of architecture just minutes away from any location in the Gainesville area. North Green Street is a treasure for everyone. The oldest house that remains today is the Robertson-Thurmond Methodist Parsonage built about 1881 to 1888, located at 529 North Green Street It was shocking to observe how often another home was being destroyed. They were being replaced by commercial buildings.

At that time, a collection began of stories and articles about all of the homes. Time was spent in the deed room, and talks with family and friends, and the search for old photographs became a passion. This author is fortunate to have a five-by-seven oak mantel featuring Ionic columns from the Oliver A. Carter house where The Times building now stands. What a treasure!

In this author's view, progress took its toll on the old homes. Progress is essential for the growth of any community, but the sad results is it sometimes destroys so much of the past. At least twenty-five homes have been lost. Many historic changes have come to North Green Street, yet today it still evokes the imagination of what it once looked like in simpler times. To capture a glimpse of time past, one must look, "Beyond the Jewels and Grandeur."

INTRODUCTION

Gainesville was approved for a charter to form a city by Georgia's Governor John Clark, on April 21, 1821. Plans were made to build the city on July 3, 1821. The land was part of land lot number 148 in the 9th District of Hall County. The land was sold to Mr. William Cobb, Mr. John Bates, Mr. John Eberhart, and Mr. John Vance by Mr. Duke Williams for one-thousand dollars. Mr. Timothy Terrell, a civil engineer in the War of 1812, was hired to survey Gainesville and set-up seventy-four lots and ten streets. A public square was reserved on a level spot in the northwest part of town.

Gainesville became a commercial and resort area, and grew from a population of about 300 in 1872 to 4,000 in 1888. When the railroad came there had to be a way to haul freight from the depot on Main Street to the square. Also, there were hot springs in the area and people who came to the city had to have a way to get to them. The answer for this problem was a street railway, first pulled by horses. The line was a mile long and built in 1874. The line was expanded in 1877 to go out Green Street to Gower Springs. Green Street became one of the most desirable places to live and raise a family.

Gainesville was almost destroyed by a fire in December 1851. Three sides of the square were burned, and both the Baptist and Presbyterian churches and courthouse were completely burned. There were two other fires in 1873 and 1876 that caused a lot of damage. Those were hard times, but the "spirit" of residents was strong.

In 1975, Green Street houses were given the distinction of being placed in the Green Street Historic District and on the National Registry. One individual this author knew who spearheaded this move was Mr. W. L. Norton, Jr. He was absolutely committed to the project's success, and he and his wife, Adelaide, and others made it happen.

The Martin-Matthews-Norton House

As one continues to stroll down the "Avenue of Green Street," there stands the Martin–Matthews–Norton house. Beneath the Tudor detailing of this home at (58) 393 Green Street are the bones of a home built by Mr. John Harrison Martin in 1910–1911. This was the first house on the property, and the second house was reconstructed in 1933 by Mr. J. D. Matthews after he purchased the property from Mrs. Mamie Martin, John Martin's widow, in 1931.

John Martin was a prominent stock dealer and the president of a bank. He was killed in 1917. His widow, Mrs. Mamie Martin, was still living at 58 Green Street (old #) in 1922 and was listed in the city of Gainesville directory. According to the *Gainesville News* on September 6, 1922, recorded in History of the Gainesville Fire Department, 1876–1939, a fire destroyed two automobiles and the barn they were stored in at 58 Green Street, where Mrs. John H.Martin lived. By 1926, listed in the Gainesville directory, she lived in the Princeton Hotel. She was living in Ware County, Georgia, with her daughter, Jonnie Martin Tigner, when she sold the 58 Green Street property to Mr. J.D. Matthews in April 1931.

Mrs. Mamie Martin was buried in 1950 by the side of her husband, Mr. John H. Martin, in the Alta Vista Cemetery.

Mr. Matthews secured a re-construction loan in 1937, and hired Mr. Levi Prater, a local carpenter to re-build the house. A look at the 1830 plat reveals that the Martin structure of the house is similar to the house located on the property today. The picturesque Tudor house is an unusual example of English Vernacular Revival style. It features two-stories with a clay tile roof, double-hung sash windows, and a stoop front. A rear extension was added in the 1970s. The house has an asymmetric façade, one front door, and a cross-gabled roof and rectangular floor plan.

Mrs. Mae Matthews, wife of Mr. J. D. Matthews, married Mr. Sam B. Ham after the death of her first husband. When Mr. Ham died, she moved to the Hunt Tower. Mrs. Matthews sold the the house to Mr. W. L. Norton on August 30, 1968. It is utilized as a commercial property, and remains in the Norton family, today.

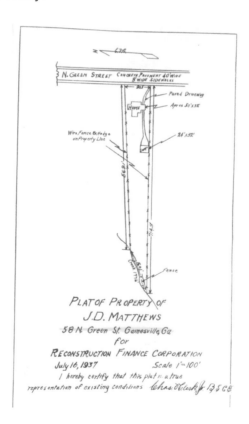

Turner–Estes House

Mr. G. E. Turner bought the land for the Turner–Estes House at 403 Green Street from Mr. Carrie B. Smith for $2,700. Mr. Turner had a house built on this lot in 1906. The house was sold to Mr. George P. Estes in 1913. Miss Helen Estes, the daughter, lived in the house until her death in 1974. She was a lovely lady and an avid member of the Daughters of the American Revolution who participated in numerous civic organizations and activities. Visitors were always welcome and graciously entertained at her home.

The Neoclassical Revival style, Queen Anne type house has a veranda on the front with fluted Corinthian columns. The ornate columns are characterized by bell-shaped capitals decorated with acanthus leaves. The porch (veranda) extends around the front and left side of the house. A semi-circular leaded-glass fan-light extends above the triple windows on the right side in front. There are three rectangular stained-glass windows located on the left side of the house, above the staircase landing between the first and second stories.

The two-story house has a hipped gable roof. There are four brick chimneys and seven fireplaces inside: one each in the entrance hall, the formal parlor, the den, and the dining room, and four upstairs. In its prime, all the fireplaces were in working order, but they are unusable today.

The dining room has a magnificent stained-glass window. As one climbs the stairway to the second floor, the triple stained-glass window (described earlier) is visible on the left above the landing between the first- and second-stories. Also, on the left side of the house is a rectangular over-light above a door that opens onto a porch. The double-sash windows on the front and sides of the house have one-over-one-lights.

An interesting feature of the second-story is a small one-over-one window at the left corner of the house. A rectangular window is located in a lengthwise position to the right of the small window.

The house has four bedrooms upstairs, with a stairway entry at the rear of the house in addition to the front. In 2004, renovations were made by the next owner. He covered the plaster walls with sheetrock and lowered the ceilings. Today, it is used as a commercial facility.

Baker–White–Sheridan House

The Baker–White–Sheridan House, located at 411 Green Street, is a Prairie-style and American foursquare type structure. The house was built by the Baker family around the turn of the twentieth century. Mr. Alex Baker was a bookkeeper for a number of years at the Downey Hospital.

The original floor plan was two unequal rooms and two-stories. It has an asymmetric façade, one front door, and a hip roof. The central projection on the second-story has three one-over-one sash windows. The hip roof dormer on the front has three diamond-pane casement windows. The windows are double-hung sash. The porch has a wood floor and brick foundation. There is one off-center, within roof surface brick chimney.

In 2005, square wooden columns with a wood balustrade were added to the porch. The rear addition has double gable porches. The roof is asphalt shingles, and the exterior of the house is covered with synthetic Masonite siding.

The house was purchased by R. G. Morgan White around 1963, and his daughter, Mrs. G. S. Sheridan, purchased it from him in 1968. Mrs. Sheridan was an outstanding educator and friend. The house is now a commercial facility occupied by Southern Reality.

Wallace House

The estimated date of construction for the Wallace House at 417 Green Street is 1900.Mr. C.P. Wallace and his second wife raised three daughters in the house. Mr. Wallace's third wife, a Mrs. Martin, outlived him, and after her death, two of his daughters, Mrs. Lucile Nuckols and Mrs. Evelyn Hughes, owned the property.

The Prairie style house is a Queen Anne type featuring a square plan with two-stories, an asymmetric façade, one front door, and a hip roof. The windows are double-hung sash. It has wide eaves with exposed rafter tails. On the north elevation, there is a side gable roof extension. There was a gable room addition (circa 1920) on the rear with four-over-four frame windows. Around 1930, a shed-roof addition was added with one-over-one wood frame windows. (One-over-one windows are half on top and half on bottom (large,full) windows). As glass became more affordable in the1890s, they became popular. Four-over-four are four on top and four on bottom; they are visible in the house photograph. The porch has a wood floor, brick foundation, and battened columns on brick piers. The house was a three-unit apartment building in 1974. Today, the house is utilized as a commercial business property.

Adams House

The Adams House located at 427 Green Street was built in 1910 and has gone through a number of renovations and owners. Some of the grantors and grantees were Mr. R. A. Roper, Mr. Z.T. Castleberry, Dr. J.D. Mauldin, Mr. W.R. Hughes, and Mr. and Mrs. J. O. Adams. It is unclear when and why the Adams family moved, but in 1927, when Mr. Adams died, Mrs. Adams moved back and lived there for a total of thirty-five years. Mrs. Adams had the house moved to the left side of the lot in 1927 and sold the other half to Mr. E. R. Barrett, who built the Hunter House. In 1974, Mr. R. E. McCallum owned Adams house.

The house is in the Folk Victorian style with a Gabled Wing Cottage type. The plan is L-shaped with one-story. Several noted renovations include a rear extension with shed-roof and dormers in the 1920s. In the 1930s, a rear service porch and shed-roof were added. The 1990s brought vinyl siding and the boarding up of some rear windows. Later, the vinyl siding was removed, repairs were made to the front porch, and asphalt shingles were added with other repairs to both the interior and exterior.

The roof type is cross-gabled with an asymmetric façade and one front door. It features a balloon frame/platform frame, brick foundation, a front veranda, clapboard and beveled siding, and double-hung sash windows. Today the house used as a commercial facility.

Swann–Hawkins–Hunter House

A Craftsman style house is located at 431 Green Street. It is a Bungalow Front Gabled type house constructed in 1930. It has an asymmetric façade, gabled-front oriented roof, asphalt shingles, and one front door. The house features nine-over-one windows with false half-timber detail and knee braces in the gables. A small front porch has brick columns with a decorative brick balustrade and flat arch fascia. The brick chimney is off-center within a roof surface.

The house was possibly built by a Mr. Freedman to rent out. The Richard Dillard family lived in the house until 1938, when Mr. Horace Hawkins bought it. Mr. Hawkins lived there with his sister, Mrs. A. H. Swann, and her two daughters. A room was added on at the rear of the house by the Swan family. Miss Sally Hunter bought the house in 1963. The house is now a commercial facility.

Finger House

The Neoclassical Revival style, Georgian type house at 439 Green Street was constructed in 1900. The house has a symmetric façade with two front doors. The plan shape is square with a balloon frame/platform frame. The house has undergone several alterations: in 1915, a rear addition; in the 1980s, an additional front entry off the front porch and, the addition of wood stairs to the second-story porch at the rear. The chimney is off-center, within a roof surface. The foundation is brick with double-hung sash windows. The porch has a wood floor, Tuscan columns on wood box pieces, and dentil detail on the cornices are impressive features.

The two-story center portico has four two-story Ionic columns covered in vinyl on top of brick pieces with granite caps, wood dentils in the cornice, and pediment gables with dentil detail. It features a small fan-light, and paired windows that flank the portico on the second-story.

Mr. John Finger lived in the house with his wife, Lottie Whelchel, and two children for a number of years. It was divided into four apartments in 1965 when Mrs. Mary C. Couch bought it. Today, the house is a utilized as a commercial facility.

Dorsey–Plaginos–Ellard House

The Colonial Revival style and I-house-Central Hallway house type located at 503 Green Street was built around 1900 by the Dorsey family. It is described in an early deed as the Dorsey Estate. In 1927, Frank Plaginos purchased the property and remodeled the house He removed the second-story porch. In 1969, P. Martin Ellard, CPA, purchased the house, and turned it into office space, and did additional remodeling.

The original two-story frame house was built in the Plantation Plain style, with porches across the front of the house. This is the only example on Green Street of this particular type of architectural design. The door of the front portico is characterized by rectangular over-and-side-lights. Ten plain columns and balustrade are additional features. The front of the first floor has two large, double-sash windows flanked on each side by two small, double-sash windows. Both the large and small windows have one-over-one lights. The front of the second floor has six one-over-one light windows with double-sashes. The foundation is brick, and the veranda is one- story wood with a hip roof.

There is only one exterior chimney. The porch has a brick foundation, concrete floor, pared square wood boxed columns and square balustrade. The recessed entry has glazed and panel doors and side-lights separated by pilasters, a frame is between door and side-lights, and solid transom. The transom has carved arch detail, and the walls and ceilings are paneled. Stationary eight-pane windows are on the rear addition basement with wood casement windows. The house is used today as a commercial, professional office

Turner–Daniel–Delong–Shelby–Mitchell House

The Neoclassical Revival house style and Queen Anne house type located at 517 Green Street was built between May 16, 1902, and July 17,1903. It was the first Queen Anne plan built in Gainesville. Dr. J. H. Daniel purchased the lot from Mr. G. F. Turner. The original architects or builders were a Mr. Butts and a Mr. Morris. Dr. Daniel lived in the house for many years. Mr. H. P. De La Pierre administered Dr. Daniel's estate and sold it to H. H. Dean on June 2,1927. Mr. Frank DeLong purchased the house in December 1927. Then in 1957, Mr. DeLong sold it to his son Harold for his young family.

The house is a very good example of Neoclassical architecture. The foundation is brick with a wrap-around porch and wood siding and sheathing. There are eight beautiful Ionic columns that support a one-story front porch with a turned balustrade. The roof is a series of gables. There is dentil work under the eaves.

The rectangular over-lights over the front door and the upper sashes of the front windows are leaded-glass. There are three small, stained-glass windows on the first floor. The remaining nine double-sash windows on the first story have one-over-one lights.

One of the noticeable features is the outside bay window upstairs formed from the curve in the right side of the house. The seven remaining windows, excluding the two arched ones on each side of the bay window, are double sash with one-over-one lights.

The entrance features a reception hall with double doors between it and the dining room, and between it and the formal parlor. There is wide cove molding throughout the house. All ceilings downstairs are eleven feet high, and those upstairs are ten feet. There are eight rooms with hardwood flooring. The only change made to the house is a large screened porch across the back made by Mr. Harold DeLong. The house is used as a commercial facility, today.

Robertson–Thurmond Methodist Parsonage

The Folk Victorian, Colonial Revival style, and Gabled Wing Cottage type house located at 529 Green Street was built between 1881 an 1888 by A. A. Marshall. The house was sold by Mr. Marshall to Mr. Willie Cheatham in 1888. Mr. T. H. Robison bought the house in 1889. In 1909, Mr. Robertson sold the house to Mr. W. H. Burt, who sold it in 1917to Dr. H. L. Rudolph. In 1935, the house was sold to Mrs. Annie Beadle, and alas in 1943, Mr. Charles J. Thurmond bought the house from the Beadle Estate. At the time of the purchase, the house had six rooms with a porch across the entire front.

Mr. John Dennis, an architect from Macon, was hired in 1951 to do extensive remodeling and additions to the house. A den and kitchen were added to the original house. The original floor plan was T-shaped and one story with an asymmetric front façade. The veranda was replaced with a stoop entry. Also, there was a side gable and a rear gable addition.

The house was purchased in 1956 by the Gainesville District North Georgia Conference of the Methodist Church. It was used as a district parsonage and was occupied by Rev. and Mrs. Robert Bridges. Rev. Bridges was the district superintendent of the Gainesville District.

The front façade is characterized by a gable containing a beveled-glass porthole window. In the last few years, many changes have been made. The house is currently used as a commercial property.

Pruitt–Wheeler–McBrayer House

The Neoclassical Revival style and Georgian type house located at 539 Green Street was constructed in 1908. Mr. J. C. Pruitt had the house built at the corner of Green Street and North Avenue. Mr. Pruitt came with his brother-in-law, C. R. Barrett, to operate a hardware store. Their hardware store was destroyed in the 1936 tornado. Judge A. C. Wheeler purchased the house in 1942. After the death of his wife, his daughter, Frances Sheeler McBrayer, became the owner.

The house has six chimneys, with two on the front side of the house and one at the rear on the side. The original floor plan was a central hallway passage with a square plan shape, two-stories, a symmetric façade, and one front door. The hip gable roof is trimmed with a pediment gable. There is a large window in the center with two-over-two lights. A semi-circular fanlight is located over the window. On each side of the center window is one small window containing nine-over-one lights. Each of the two gables on each side of the small window contains a window with twelve lights, in addition to a semicircular fanlight. The gables on both the right and left side of the house contain a window with one-over-one lights.

Pocket Doors

Pocket doors were very popular during the Victorian Era. This house has beautiful pocket doors. These doors took up less space and made a room look larger or smaller when they were opened or closed. The doors were slid into pockets inside the wall. They were plain or decorated.

The central two-story portico has six fluted Ionic columns surrounded by smaller ones, rectangular over-lights-and-side-lights features of the front door, and Dentil molding is a feature of both stories. The balcony of the second-story and the porch of the first-story have a turned balustrade. Large pilasters are located on each side of the front door. The interior details of the three front rooms include paneling, wainscoting, and other turn-of-the-century features.

The front of the first story and the sides of both stories contain double-sash windows with one-over-one lights, and the front of the second-story contains double-sash windows with twelve-over-one lights. The porthole windows are located on each side of the double-doors that open onto the balcony of the second floor. The left side of the second-story has a large, rectangular stained-glass window. The right side of the first story contains three rectangular stained-glass windows located directly above a larger double-sash window with one-over-one lights. All are located in a slightly curved section of the wall.

There is a porch that extends one-third on the left and one-half on the right side. An open carport is on the right side, and a screened porch is on the left side. A latticework porch is at the rear of the house. The house had a rear gable roof addition in the 1920s. In the 1950s, a two-story rear flat roof and a rear flat service porch enclosure were added. The house is currently used as a commercial, professional building.

Riley–Newman–Quinlan–Jones House

The house located at 605 Green Street is a beautiful example of a Neoclassical Revival style and Georgian type house constructed in 1903 and 1904. In 1897, Professor and Mrs. Madison Monroe Riley moved to Gainesville from Greenville, South Carolina. Professor Riley bought one-third interest in Brenau College. He also purchased property from Mr. S. C. Dunlap and Mr. H. H. Dean for $1,300. In 1917, Mr. Harvey M. Newman, a dry goods merchant, bought the house. He glassed in part of the veranda in 1920. Mr. and Mrs. Leslie Quinlan moved from Philadelphia, Pennsylvania, in 1936. He established the Owen Osborne Hosiery Mill, and at that time, they bought the house.

The major restoration of the house took place in 1939 when Mr. Quinlan added Doric columns to the front of the house and bathrooms in each of the five upstairs bed rooms. Mr. and Mrs. David Jones bought the house from the Quinlan family in 1974. The Quinlan family had lived in the house for thirty-seven years.

The outside of the house is a balloon frame and platform style with white clapboard covered with aluminum siding. The foundation is brick. The house features a hip gabled roof. The entrance of the front façade is distinguished by a two-story portico, four Doric columns, double front doors with rectangular beveled-glass over-lights and side-lights, a balcony, and a pediment.

The original double-sash windows of the front and second story have one-over-one lights. The windows in the Miami room have small panes. The house has two staircases, one in the hall and another near the kitchen. There were eight rooms downstairs that included a dining room, a living room, a parlor, a kitchen, a breakfast room, a den, a playroom, and a Miami room. Double mahogany sliding doors lead into the entrance to the den, dining room, and living room.

Other outstanding features include four beveled-glass windows in the dining room and two original chandeliers, one in the dining room and the other in the hallway. In addition, there are three arched stained-glass windows above the staircase landing between the first and second stories.

There are six fireplaces, one in the parlor, the living room, and the den, and three up stairs. The house has a total of six thousand feet. The floors are original and are made from heart of pine. The house is used as a commercial property.

Charters–Smith House

The Neoclassical Revival style, Georgian house type at 625 Green Street was constructed in 1906 and has a special memory for this author. It was the family home of Mrs. Charters Smith Embry, a dear and longtime friend. The house was built by her grandfather, Colonel William H. Charters, a prominent attorney and solicitor of North Georgia. Colonel Charters had the house built for his lovely bride, Isabelle Price Charters, a Brenau student. She was the organizing regent of Colonel William Candler Chapter, NSDAR. The house remained unaltered for seventy-years.

The house has clapboard siding with a wide, covered, semi-circular veranda. The small porch on the left side of the house is an entrance to the back sitting room. Six fluted Corinthian columns; rectangular beveled, leaded-glass over-lights and side-lights; a central; two-story portico; two porthole windows; lintel on the second floor; and dentil work on the first and second stories are fabulous features of the beautiful house.

The house has a hip gabled roof, four chimneys, and four fireplaces, one in each front room on either side of the house and two upstairs. On either side of the corners of the attic which has dormer windows are two pilasters. The two porthole windows are in the second story; the remaining double-sash windows of the first and second-stories contain nine-over-nine lights.

The plan shape is rectangular with a symmetric façade with one entry door. One unusual feature of the entrance hall is the hardwood floor outlined with a Greek key design in darker wood. Wide archways frame the parlor on either side of the hall. Three high windows in the room beyond the right parlor have rose-colored stained-glass.

The stairway runs the width of the rear hall and has three landings. Off the second landing is an inset landing that features a beveled stained-glass window with flower designs. Other outstanding architectural features are Adam design mantels, eight heavy panel doors, and wide molding. Today, the house is used as a commercial facility.

Walking up this unique stairway in this fabulous house is exhilarating. One is a bit winded when reaching the top, but just looking out the window is an outstanding treat

Dunlap–Burroughs House

The Craftsman style, Georgian type house located at 635 Green Street was built in 1912. Mr. Samuel C. Dunlap built the house for his son, Samuel C. Dunlap, Jr. The timber from the house was cut from the Thompson Place, the ancestral farm. On August 20,1917, Perl T. Adams purchased the house and completed the upstairs. Mr. Dunlap bought the house back. When he died, Mrs. Corrine Riley Burroughs bought the house. In 1974, the house was owned by Mr. Samuel Riley Dunlap.

The front porch wraps to the north with a brick foundation, concrete steps with granite-capped brick, apron walls, and a wood floor. It has granite-capped brick pieces with single square wood columns, triple at the corners, and half-wall balustrade. The entry has a beveled-glass door with a large single pane, beveled glass-sidelights, and a transom covered with aluminum. The Palladian dormer on the façade has stationary windows, and the center has an arched transom.

The rear addition has one-over-one windows. In 1980, a flat-roofed side room on the south elevation was added. In 1990, a rear entry with a paneled door, four lights, and panel side-lights and an arched fan-light transom were added. The windows are double-hung sash, flat-headed and one-over-one rectangular. There are three chimneys, a balloon frame/platform frame construction, and vinyl and aluminum siding. The house is currently used as a commercial property.

Boone–Garner–Lathem House

The High Victorian Eclectic style, Queen Anne type house located at 380 Green Street has a square plan shape, an asymmetric façade, and one front glazed and paneled door with leaded-glass. The house was constructed in 1885. The original owner of the house, Mr. Joseph Radcliff Boone, was a large landowner and builder. He was the first stockholder in the First National Bank (Regions Bank), an ordinary, and a city clerk. The house was purchased by Mr. Ed Barrett in 1915, who added rooms on the rear of the house. Dr. Raleigh Garner lived in the house from 1930 to 1970. In 1970, Mr. William L. Norton, Jr., bought the house and remodeled it for his law office.

The front veranda wraps around on the south elevation and has wood floors, turned posts, and swan brackets. The railings have narrow square posts topped with square panels with quatrefoil detail. The roof is a shed on the end and hip in the corner.

The second-story porch is recessed under a gable projection and turned posts. The balusters are in a pinwheel pattern and have quatrefoil panels at the center, and the pinwheel gable has the sunburst detail. The house has a balloon frame/platform frame with vinyl and aluminum siding.

The gabled front projection includes fish scale shingles and stained-glass windows. The fascia has stick detail, scrolled brackets, and medallions. The windows on the left side are one-over-one sash on the first-story and paired on the second story, with fluted surrounds and rondelle (circular) corner pieces. Other windows have plain surrounds and stacked cornices. The house is currently a commercial property.

Judge William L. Norton, Malissa, sister, Frank K. Norton

Judge William L. Norton, Jr., Malissa, sister, and Mr. Frank K. Norton

In 1968, Judge William L. and Adelaide Gregory Norton spearheaded the movement to save the historic houses on Green Street. This resulted in the formation of the Hall County Historical Society. Judge Norton purchased the Boone–Garner–Lathem House for his law office.

Lathem–Barrett–Moore House

The Folk Victorian, Colonial Revival style house and Central Hallway Cottage type house at 404 was originally constructed in 1890. Land records trace back to 1885. It has a rectangular plan with one-story. The house has one front door with a symmetric façade. The original floor plan had a central hallway (passage) with more than two rooms. According to a 1974 survey, it originally had five rooms with twelve-foot ceilings.

Mr. George Lathem owned the house from 1907 to 1917 and then sold it to Mr. and Mrs. Carl Barrett, who owned it for about twenty years. Mr. John Moore was the next owner and rented it to Mr. C. J. Clever, who was the Gainesville City School superintendent until 1943. In 1943, Mr. Robert Lee Moore bought the house. Then in 1946, Mr. Robert Lee Moore did major restoration work. Mr. W. F. Hennens bought the house in 1960.

The original veranda, from 1890, was removed and replaced with a stoop. The house has vinyl siding with rear gable extensions. The roof type is side-oriented with asphalt shingles. The type of house construction is a balloon frame and platform frame. The windows are double-hung sash.

The gable roof over the entry bay features an entry with a paneled door with five light transom, fluted pilasters and dentil detail. The front stoop has a brick floor, paired square columns, and stacked fascia with a hip roof. The south side rear appears to be original to the house; a side entrance is newer. The house has a brick foundation and a partial basement. Today, the house is used as a professional facility.

Hosch House

The Hosch House constructed in 1907 by Mr. and Mrs. John Hosch is a Neoclassical Revival style house with an American Foursquare Building type. The original floor plan has two-unequal rooms (more than two rooms). It has a square plan shape with two-stories. It features one front door with an asymmetric façade, and the door is glazed and paneled with a stained-glass transom. The windows are double-hung sash (flat-headed, one-over-one rectangular).

A two-story hip roof projection is on the rear of the north and south elevations, and on the rear of the house, a one-story hip roof extension/addition is at the rear. The two-story hip roof was slate until recently, when it had to be replaced. An entry from the side wrap porch opens into the south elevation projection and has a glazed and paneled door and stained-glass transom. There are decorative wood carved appliqué on the second-story façade.

The placement of the chimney is off-center, within a roof surface, and the type of construction is a balloon and platform frame. The foundation is brick, and the veranda on the front of the house end partially wraps around both sides. The porch features fluted Doric columns turned balustrade, wood floor, and brick steps with an apron.

There are three outbuildings, and some of them date to 1898. The garage is a historic, two-bay frame with hip roof, decorative metal shingles, and paneled doors with a multi-pane window at the top. The barn was constructed by Mr. John H. Hosch in 1898. It features a front gable with a projecting loft roof supported by large braces. The office is a small, one-story, frame-side gable with beveled siding and stone chimney. One gable fronts Green Street, with an arched batten style door and six-over-six paired windows. A built-in kitchen was recently added from a portion of the original back porch.

This house and property is still in the Hosch family. The owners are Mr. and Mrs. Heyward Hosch. It has been this author's joy and privilege to visit with Heyward and Marian often, with time spent spinning family tales. Also, I am proud to call Marian Martin Hosch a cousin and Heyward Hosch, a true gentleman and friend.

Mantels in the house feature free-standing Ionic columns.

32.

The Hosch Family

The Hosch family. *Left to right*: Angeline Braselton Hosch, Heyward C. Hosch, Heyward C. Hosch, Jr. (child), and John Harrison Hosch(first owner).

The Cabin at the Hosch House.

The 1898 Barn.

The cabin at the Hosch house.
The 1898 barn.

Nalley–Martin House

The Nalley-Martin house is one of the last great houses erected on Green Street. This Federal Revival style and Georgian type house was constructed in 1938 by Mr. Ray Knickerbocker. It is one of the newest homes on Green Street. The original owner was Mr. C. V. Nalley, who raised his family in the house. He raised five sons and one daughter in the house. Mrs. J. H. Martin purchased the house after Mr. Nalley's death. The present owner is Mr. Frank Norton. Today, the house is used as a commercial business office.

The house has one front door and a symmetric façade. The roof is a hip roof, and the plan shape is square. The front façade of the two-story house is characterized by rectangular sidelights and beveled glass in the front door. Two large Doric columns extend the height of both stories. Dentil blocks are features of the overhang and under the side of the large triangular gable on the second story. Two gables are present on the roof.

The large, two-story rear addition is larger than the original house, post-1974, and mimics the original house. The house is brick and has been painted white. The double-sash windows of the first story contain eight-over-twelve lights. Those on the first-story contain twelve-over-twelve lights—The second-story has a window above the front door and feature a semicircular fanlight and rectangular sidelights. A plain balustrade is in front of the central window, and brackets support the extension in front of the window. The two dormer windows in the upper gable have six-over-six lights.

There are two brick chimneys on each side of the house, and they extend above the hip gable roof. The left side chimney is free-standing. The porch on the right side of the house features twelve small Doric columns, three at each front corner; the remaining six are in groups of two. There is a balcony surrounded by wrought iron on the top of the porch.

Classical symmetry details are found in the interior of the house. When I recently visited the house, I was told that the wallpaper in the entry is original to the house. On each side of the entrance hall, rounded arch cornice is present. In the parlor, wainscoting is featured.

Smith–Palmour–Estes House

The original owner of this Queen Anne style and type house was Mr. James Whitfield Smith and was built around 1888. According to a 1974 survey with information from his daughter, Miss Ruth Smith, Mr. Smith was a cotton broker from West Point, Georgia. His father was a surgeon who had moved to Gainesville for his health. Mr. James W. Smith was the father of Mr. Sidney Oslin Smith, an insurance executive, and the grandfather of Judge Sidney O. Smith. In 1925, Dr. W. A. Palmour bought the house for $12,000 when the Smith family moved to Atlanta. In 1941, Mrs. C. V. Nalley bought the house for $5,200. Mr. Marvin Lawson bought the house for $7,000 in 1942. Then, Mr. Henry Estes bought the house in 1944 for $12,000. This was a bit of old-fashioned horse trading. It is also interesting to note that the original Mr. Smith, owner, planted the tree in the front yard.

The front of the house at 446 Green Street has Eastlake and Victorian details. The front porch (veranda) projects slightly to the north end of the façade and then wraps to the side turned posts, bracket details, sawn balustrade, gingerbread detail, carved modillions, and gable over the front and south elevation entries are features. The second-story balcony has turned posts and sawn balustrade. It has a glazed and paneled door with stained-glass lights.

This is one of the most photographed and talked about houses on North Green Street.

There are two bay windows on the first-story, one to the left of the house in the formal parlor, and one in the sitting room in the center of the house. In addition to the double-sash windows with one-over-one lights, the second-story has the same type of double-sash windows. stained-glass windows and a pediment attic gable have a space with three small windows with nine panes each. In the gable over the second-story porch, and in the gable dormer at the top of the hip roof, is a corner turret–projecting bay window on the south elevation. Details in the projecting front gable include fish scale shingles, sunburst, and stained-glass.

There are three brick chimneys that are off-center within the roof surface. One is on each side of the house, and one is at the rear. The construction is a balloon frame and platform frame with an exterior wood weatherboard/clapboard/beveled siding. The windows are double-hung sash, flat-headed, one-over-one, and rectangular with fixed, flat-headed, rectangular designs.

The beautiful reception hall greets guests as they enter the house. In the 1974 survey, the stairway was moved from the reception hall to the middle room, and a side entrance was added to the room. This renovation took place in 1910. Later, a one-story historic porch was enclosed at the rear of the house. The beautiful oak stairway in the middle of the house with four turns and graining leads to the second-story.

There are other features of the house such as wainscoting in one front room, window and door frames with medallions, very ornate Victorian mantels, wide-board floors upstairs, and a window seat in the dining room. This house is special to this author. A dear friend, Heneretta Estes, grew up in this house. There are beautiful stairways and handmade mantels. A fantastic feature is the handmade door hinges.

Burns-Moss- Palmour House

The Colonial Revival style and Georgian type house located at 454 Green Street was built in 1924. It was designed by Mr. John Cherry from Atlanta, Georgia. The builder was Mr. Ervin Ledford. The original owner was Mr. Hubert Barnes. Mr. Thomas S. Moss bought the house in 1955. A local architect, Mr. Garland Reynolds, bought the house in 1970 and renovated it for his office. Later, the law firm of Palmour and Palmour had their office in the house.

The house has three chimneys with a balloon frame and platform frame construction type, a brick foundation, and vinyl/aluminum siding. The front portico is one-story and partial wood. The windows are double-hung sash, flat-headed, six-over-six, and rectangular.

The entry consists of a paneled door with leaded-glass side-lights and a flat-arch transom. There are unusual arched windows on the façade. The first-story has round-headed sash façade and keystone detail in the surround, flanked by arched shutters with crescent cutouts. The porch has paired fluted Corinthian columns, single pilasters, stacked cornice, and turned roof balustrade. The porch extends to the patio on each side. Modillion detail is in the eaves. There is a recessed side entry on the south elevation. The house is a commercial property.

Barrett–Whitehead House

The Prairie Craftsman style house located at 466 Green Street was constructed in 1930. The house is an unusual example of the Prairie style in Gainesville. The contractor was Mr. Levi Prater. The two-story, rectangular plan features an asymmetric façade and a hip roof. From the 1974 survey, the original owners were Mr. and Mrs. E. R. Barrett. It was built on the home site of former Georgia Governor Allen D. Candler. In 1959, Mr. and Mrs. Carl Whitehead, Jr., purchased the property.

The roof is composition shingle and asphalt shingles, off-center, within the roof surface The type of construction is a balloon frame and platform frame. The foundation and the exterior is brick-running bond and veneer with machine-made stretchers.

The porch is enclosed brick piers with concrete caps and square brick columns. Concrete caps are at the top with arched openings. The triple windows on the façade (only the second-story is visible) has twelve-over-one sash flanked by nine-over-one sash and eight-over-one sash. stained-glass is in the stairway on the north elevation. There is a double frame and modillion detail in the eaves.

There is a two-bay garage in the rear with a brick gable front and hinged doors with an entrance on both Green and Candler Streets. Today, the house is utilized as a professional office.

Garner–Hulsey House

The Neoclassical Revival style and Georgian type house located at 616 Green Street was constructed in 1925. It has a rectangular plan shape and two-stories. There is one front door and a symmetric façade. From a 1974 survey, a Mrs. Garner had the house built identical to one next door, where Dr. John Hulsey grew up. Dr. Hulsey owned the house in 1974.

There façade features a hip roof dormer. The windows are double-hung sash, flat-headed, one-over-one, and rectangular. The windows are paired and have lowered shutters on the façade; three fixed panes are in the dormer. The porch wraps on the south elevation and extends porte-cochère on the north elevation. It has paired Corinthian columns with rosette detail, turned balustrade, and double fascia with dentil detail. The house has a brick foundation and concrete steps with concrete-capped brick apron walls.

The porch projects slightly at the entry bay and has a gable pediment and a second-story door to the balcony. The front door has one beveled-glass with leaded-glass side-lights and fan-light. The second-story door to the balcony has one glass pane and is flanked by leaded-glass side-lights.

From the 1974 survey, the house was built from heart of pine and was air-dried for two years. It has maple floors and brick trim, and the stair rail is birch-stained mahogany. There is a two-bay garage at the rear of the side drive. Also, the house features a hip roof, weatherboard, and paired hinged doors that are paneled with two rows of glass panes. Today, the house is used as a commercial building.

Adams–Smith–Edmonson–Ward House

According to the 1974 survey, the house at 634 Green Street was constructed in 1915.The contractor was Mr. Levi Prater and was built for Mr. and Mrs. John Adams. It was a copy of one Mr. Adams had built in 1909 on Brenau Avenue. Around 1920, the house was purchased by the Sidney O. Smith family. Later, the house was owned by Mr. and Mrs. J. B. Edmonson. In the 1940s, Mr. and Mrs. Bryce Ward bought the house.

The house is a Neoclassical Revival style and a New South type. The plan is an irregular shape with two-stories. The construction type is a balloon frame/platform frame. The foundation is stone with exterior vinyl and aluminum siding. The windows are double-hung sash, flat-headed, one-over-one, and rectangular. The porch is a partial one and wraps to the north elevation with a hip roof. It has a wood floor, fluted Ionic columns, turned balustrade, and double fascia (vinyl covered). The steps are made of single granite blocks with granite apron walls.

The house has one door and an asymmetric façade. The projection on the façade has a decorative stained-glass transom with wreath detail and has a wood surround with a stacked header and flat arch detail. The stained-glass window on the south elevation has some wreath detail. The stained-glass window on the north elevation has Art Nouveau detail.

The original floor plan was two unequal rooms (more than two rooms). The hip roof is composite and asphalt shingles. There are three brick chimneys. This author had such good times visiting a friend when a college student at Brenau. It was a lovely and comfortable house, but sometimes it was a bit too cold.. The house is now a commercial facility.

Dixon–Rudolph House

The English Vermicular Revival house located at 700 Green Street was designed by Mrs. John Rudolph. The house was constructed by her mother, Mrs. Annie Perry Dixon, as a home for herself and Dr. and Mrs. John Rudolph. In a 1974 survey, the house was owned by Dr. and Mrs. Rudolph.

The original floor plan was irregular with two-stories. It has an asymmetric façade. The roof is gable-side-oriented and cross-gable. The roof is composite and asphalt shingle. The two chimneys of fieldstone are off-center, within the roof surface. The foundation is stone, with features on the exterior weatherboard, clapboard, beveled siding, and wood-half timbers. The one-story front stoop is partial wood. The windows are double-hung sash, flat-headed, six-over-one, rectangular and double hung sash, flat- headed four-over one rectangular.

Additional physical features are false half-timber detail in the gable. It has a quadruple stained-glass window on the façade with a crest-like pattern in the lower windows, as well as a painted arch pattern in the flat-headed transom. The single gable on the north elevation has been enclosed and is now used as the entry with a batten-style door. There is knee brace detail in the eaves. The house was converted into a restaurant facility some years ago.

Jackson–Walters–Parker–Jackson House

The house located at 718 Green Street is a Neoclassical Revival style and Georgia house type built in 1909. The house was designed by a Mr. Patterson and a Mr. Harrison. The original floor plan had two unequal rooms (more than two rooms) and a rectangular plan shape. The house has one front door and a symmetric façade. There are three fireplaces.

The hip roof is composition and asphalt shingle with three brick chimneys. The house has a balloon frame/platform frame with a brick foundation, and the exterior is wood weatherboard clapboard and beveled siding. The front veranda is one-story wood with a hip roof. The front portico is two-stories and partial wood with a gable. The balcony front is one story and partial wood. The windows are double-hung sash, flat-headed, six-over-one, and rectangular. The door that opens onto the balcony of the second story has a rectangular over-light and two small double-sash windows on each side with six-over-one lights.

The first-story porch wraps at the north and south elevations, and is partially enclosed at the south elevation, and features Ionic columns, a wood floor, concrete steps with concrete-capped brick apron walls. The centered balcony tops the first-story porch and has a turned balustrade, and low wood-paneled piers. The two-story pediment gable portico was added in 1914. The portico has fluted Ionic columns, gable pediment with dentil detail, and an arched fan-light with scalloped and keystone detail.

The entry has a paneled door with leaded-glass side-lights and a leaded-glass transom. There is a two-story side projection on the north and south elevation with two historic two-story extensions on the rear. In the 1974 survey, a garage at the rear of the house existed, but it is no longer is standing. Two non-historic office buildings are located at the rear of the property.

The interior has eighteenth-century mantels, pocket doors, and a chair rail in the dining room. The original owner of the house was Mr. Patrick Newton Parker, who moved from Homer, Georgia, to Gainesville around 1890. He married Clara Saranel Abbot of Duluth. Mr. Parker was the mayor of Gainesville during the 1903 tornado. He served as the chairman of the First Methodist Church Building Committee in 1906. Their daughter was the author of, *The Seven Ages of Woman*.

Mr. Felix Jackson bought the house from Mr. Parker in 1914. It is interesting to note that the reason the family moved to Gainesville was for his wife's health, and he wanted his son to be educated at Riverside Military Academy. He built Gainesville's first skyscraper, the Jackson Building, in 1915. After his wife's death in 1921, he moved to Philadelphia and entered the shipping business. In 1974, his son Walton and wife, Sally Mae Holman Jackson, were living in the house. The house is currently used as a commercial/business facility.

Quillian–Brown–Jackson House

The Colonial Revival Style and Georgia Federal Type house was built in 1911, and is located 736 Green Street. The original owner of the house was Mr. George Quinlan. The house originally had five rooms and was built in 1897. Two of the rooms from the original house were used for the living in the house built by Mr. Quinn. Mrs. F. P. Brown, stepdaughter, inherited the house in 1929, and made changes to the porch and some of the rooms. The porch which extended all the way around the house was removed and the morning and afternoon porches were added to the sides of the house. These porches built in 1929 extend from north to south elevations and have Tuscan columns and turned balustrade. Also, a partition was removed between a bedroom and parlor to make a large living room. The windows are triple on the first-story façade and paired on the second-story. The two-story roof extensions on the rear are historic.

Mr. and Mrs. Walton Jackson, newlyweds, bought the house from Mrs. Brown and made additional changes. The date is unknown, but was possibly in the 1950 or 1960s. The ceilings were lowered from sixteen feet to fourteen feet, the archway was squared and several fireplaces were closed. The house was purchased in 1973 by Mr. and Mrs. Troy Millican. They "fell in love" with the house and planned to work on needed restorations.

The house has a central one-story portico with four Doric columns and an arched door. Other features include a rectangular over-light, and one rectangular side-light. I the first-story, there is a group of three one-over-one windows on either side of two small windows. The second-story has two larger windows on either side of two smaller windows.

The house has a square floor plan with two-stories and a symmetric façade. The hip roof is composite shingle/asphalt shingle. The type of construction is a balloon frame/platform and platform frame and a brick foundation. The chimneys are brick off-center, within a roof surface-off center. The front one-stoop is partial wood with a hood; the side veranda is one-with a hip roof and partial wood; and the rear stoop is one-story partial wood with a hood. The flared hoods are supported by paired Tuscan columns on the façade and the real elevation. The house was altered again in 1990 vinyl siding added.

The house had six rooms downstairs, a kitchen, dining room, living room (both with closed fireplaces), a den, playroom, and a bathroom. There were six rooms upstairs, and a bathroom. It was ideal for a growing family. The house has been altered to accommodate commercial needs.

Other features of the house include sixteen-inch molding downstairs, a custom-made Curtis mantel in the living room, baseboard with capped molding, oak hardwood floors, and oak wainscoating in the living room, and a custom-made front door.

This beautiful house has weathered many changes. From an architectural point of view, it has seen a metamorphosis from a Victorian style that featured a wraparound porch to the Colonial Revival style observed today. It now serves as a professional/commercial facility.

The first floor has back stairs that lead to Upstairs.

This is a beautiful Pocket Door.

The Tuscan column is a version of the Greek Doric column. The main characteristic of the Tuscan column is its simplicity. They can be observed on the front and back entry. Ionic columns are visible on the morning and evening porches.

EVENING PORCH

FRONT ENTRY

BACK ENTRY

MORNING PORCH

Longstreet–Newton House

The 1911 Neoclassical Revival style and American Foursquare type house was originally owned by Mrs. Helen D. Longstreet, the second wife of General James Longstreet. She was a former postmistress of Gainesville. She lost her money fighting to keep Georgia Power from damming Tallulah Falls, and she lost her house in 1911 to secure a debt to Southern Life Insurance Company in Montgomery, Alabama. In 1916, Mr. Charles Newton, a banker and surveyor, bought the house. Mr. Newton added a second story to accommodate his large family. After his death in 1965, the house was sold to Mr. Rafe Banks, who lived in the house next door.

The house has two-stories with an asymmetric façade. It was originally one story, and the second-story addition was added after 1916. The house has undergone a number of changes. The roof is composition and asphalt shingle with several brick chimneys. It has a balloon frame/platform frame construction with a brick foundation and vinyl and aluminum siding. The front veranda was one full story and wood until a few years ago, when a second story was added with railings all the way across. The windows are double-hung sash, flat-headed, one-over-one, and rectangular.

An interesting historical feature of the house according to a 1974 survey is that Mrs. Longstreet held Catholic church services in her basement, where the fireplaces were built to resemble an altar. The basement was used for a number of years before a Catholic church was built. Today, the house is used as a wellness spa.

Miller–Banks House

The house located at 756 Green Street was built in 1912 and was first owned by Mr. William Abner Miller. The house was built by Mr. Levi Prater. Mr. and Mrs. Miller lived in the house until 1916, when they sold it to Mr. and Mrs. Rafe Banks, Sr. The house style is Neoclassical Revival and Georgian Building type.

The white clapboard house has a central, two-story portico with four large Ionic columns at the front, which are interspersed and flanked with smaller Doric columns that extend along the porch on the left side of the house. The floor plan is a rectangular shape with one front door and a symmetric façade. The hip roof is composite and asphalt shingle. The three chimneys are brick, and the windows are double-hung sash, flat-headed, and one-over-one rectangular.

The front veranda is one-story and full wood with a hip roof. It has concrete steps with stone aprons, Tuscan columns, turned balustrade, and fascia with dentil details. The front portico is two-story, partial wood, and gabled. The side porte-cochère is one story and partial wood. It wraps to the north elevation with enclosures at the rear of the north elevation and extends at the south elevation. The center portico has a pediment gable at three center bays.

The front balcony is one-story and partial wood. The second-story balcony spans three center bays and has wood floors and turned balustrade. Projectiles cover the first-story porch and second-story balcony. Fluted Ionic columns with egg and dart and shell detail, stacked fascia, and dentil detail are special features of the house.

The entry is made up of double doors with a single panel and single pane in each, flanked by a sash-window with a diamond pattern in the upper sash and topped by a pane transom. The upstairs balcony has a glazed and paneled door with a transom. The windows on the gable roof dormer have a diamond-pattern sash. The side entry at the basement has a Tudor-like arched French door with a flared arch hood.

There is a two-bay garage at the rear of the side door, as well as a basement built into a hill with stone walls exposed on three sides. The garage doors are paneled with multiple lights on the top row. In 1939, a studio was added to the second-story. The upstairs wing was added later, and a side veranda was enclosed with glass. Mr. Ervin Ledford was an architect who helped with the addition, but no date is known.

A feature of the house as one enters is a stairway with two landings. At the landing between the two are two stained-glass windows. There are also stained-glass windows in the dining room. One of the walls in the dining room is slightly curved. Today, the house is utilized as a business/ commercial property.

Glossary

abacus	A slab on top of the capital of a column.
appliqué	A decoration or an ornament made by cutting pieces of one material and adding them to the surface of another.
balustrade	A rail and the row of balusters or posts that support it.
column	There are three types of columns.
	Corinthian — This column is the most ornate, and the proportions are more-slender than the Doric or the Ionic. It is characterized by a bell-shaped capital decorated with acanthus leaves.
	Doric — The oldest and simplest of the three orders of classical Greek architecture is characterized by heavy columns with plain shaped capitals and no lace.
	Ionic — The columns are more slender than the Doric, but less than the Corinthian. It has columns topped by capitals with scroll shaped ends called volutes.
colonnade	A row or series of columns.
Classical architecture	Based on examples of architecture from ancient Greece and Rome.
cornice	The molding at the top of the walls of a room, between the walls and the ceiling.
dentil	A block-shaped element of classical crown moldings. It is a series of rectangular blocks. A molding or projection beneath a cornice.
façade	The face of a building.
fanlight	A half-circle window, often with sash bars arranged like a fan.

faux	Not real, false.
Federal	An architectural style, mostly from the 1700s to the 1830s.
finial	An ornament fixed to the top of an arch or ached structure.
gable	A simple roof shape which creates a triangular end wall.
Greek revival	A style popular between 1830 and 1880s. This style was the first of the Victorian style to develop. It was characterized by pointed-arch windows and very steep roofs. It did not need decorations to achieve its architectural effects.
lintel	The horizontal beam over a window or door.
loggia	An open-sided roofed gallery or arcade along the front or side of a building, often on an upper level, and often overlooking a courtyard.
Masonite	Type of fiberboard used for instillation, paneling or partition.
medallion	A large medal object used as a decoration.
modillion	An ornamented bracket used in a series under a cornice.
palladian	Architecture characteristic of mid-eighteenth-century Geek influence.
pediment	A wide, low-pitched gable surrounding a façade of a building in the Grecian style; the element is used in architecture and decoration.
portico	A covered entry or porch supported on at least one side by columns.
porte-cochère	A carriage entrance leading through a building or wall into an enclosed courtyard.
pilaster	A thickening in a wall that lends extra stiffness to the structure.
Quatrefoil	A flower ornament used as a decoration in architecture.
style	Exterior decoration or ornamentation of a house.
turned balustrade	This is a "gingerbread" detail. A rail and the row of balusters or posts.
type	The overall form of the house, outline of the original or main part, and general layout of interior rooms.
volute	A spiral, scroll-like ornament like on an Ionic capital.
vaulted	Spanned by an arch or series of aches.

(Consult Page 60 for Definition of Columns).

Corinthian   Doric   Ionic

Appendix I

- Architecture style defines the exterior of the house.
- Architecture type defines the interior of the house.
- A house with one style may have a different type.

Style (Exterior of House)

Craftsman style: The Craftsman is simple in design with elements of mostly wood; wood exterior, wide and overhanging eaves, large front and side porches with square columns, and square railings. The inside had hardwood construction. Another feature is casement windows, windows with multiple panes in the top sash and one lower pane sash. The idea of bringing in windows, doors and other open interior finishes allowed natural beauty to be present. The Craftsman style was popular from about 1905 until the 1940s.

Colonial Revival style: This is a symmetrically arranged rectangular plan, often with a wing or garage extending from one end. An emphasis on the entry is important with attention to pediments, pilasters, fanlights, and other decorative features. Another feature is detail given to windows with many panes (six, eight, etc.) in each sash. This style was popular during the first half of the twentieth century.

English Vernacular style: In this style, porches do not exist or are small. The roofs are steeply pitched cross gable roofs, and the front often has a front-facing gable. Several English designs appear in this style. Some common features found in this design are false half timbering, large masonry chimneys, and windows with a diamond pattern. This style was popular from around the turn of the twentieth century until the 1940s.

Folk Victorian style: This style features a combination of Victorian and Romantic classic English Cottage styles and features of the American Homestead style. It seems to display some Queen Anne features, but with more modest decorations and far less expense for those who could not afford to invest in more elaborate and higher styles.

Neoclassical Revival style: This is an architectural style based on the architecture of Rome and Greece. A revival in the eighteenth and nineteenth centuries in the decorations became characterized by order, symmetry, and simplicity of style.

Prairie style: The intent behind this design was to bring people closer to the nature world. It was popularized by Frank Lloyd in 1893. The house can be boxy and symmetrical or low-asymmetrical. The concept characteristic of the home is a box subdivided into smaller boxes. The exterior can contain a single-story porch with massive supports, and it is stylized by floral and circular geometric terra-cotta or masonry ornamentation around doors, windows, and cornices.

Prairie Craftsman style: This style is simple in design with elements of mostly wood exterior, shake roofing, and hardwoods inside. It has the characteristics of the Prairie style of a box that brings nature closer.

Plantation Plain style: This is a version of the I House, but with an integral one-story rear shed. It contains two or three rooms and an under-porch.

Queen Anne style: This style is the most ornate of the Victorian-era styles. It became stylish in about 1880. It features asymmetrical massing, long wraparound porches beadwork, and a turret or round shape

Type (Interior of House)

American Foursquare: This type is characterized by four rooms on each story with no hallway. The house usually opens into a room housing the stairway.

Bungalow type: This is usually one or one and a half stories with dormers and a sloped roof. It is simple in design, is constructed from wood or brick, and lacks lots of ornamental features. Its popularity began in California in the late 1800s.

Colonial Revival type: The interior of this type of house is filled with decorative details.

Gabled Wing Cottage type: This is also known as the Gabled Front and Wing. It is a three or four room house with an L or T intersecting roof.

Georgian House Building type: The Georgian House is two-stories and has the same characteristics as the Georgian Cottage. The house has a hall with rooms on either side. It is two rooms deep. It is usually square.

New South type: This type has a hipped roof and projecting gable. It also has a central hallway. This house type was ideal for those with moderate incomes. They were mainly constructed between 1890 and the 1920s.

Queen Anne House type: The floor plan had no central hallway, and the rooms are asymmetrically arranged. Chimneys were found in the interior. The roof is hipped or pyramidal and had a square main mass with projecting gables on the front and the sides. This type of cottage was built from the 1880s to the 1890s.

Appliqué on the Hosch House

Appendix II

Houses torn down with new structures built in their location, from The Times to Holly Drive; at least seven were torn down. Parking lot space was used when others were torn down.

- The Times, located at the Oliver A. Carter home place (late 1960s).
- The house designed by Mr. Jack Bailey in the 1980s, located at 615, where Sandy Beaver lived. (The Beaver House was moved to the back of the lot and soon after burned down).
- The Hall County Government and the First Baptist Church are located between Ridgewood Avenue and Holly Drive.

From the Gainesville post office to the civic center, four homes were lost.

- The parking lot for the Quinlan Art Center replaced the Redwine House at 502.
- The Quinlan Art Center replaced the Kimbrough House at 514.
- A small office building replaced the John Hulsey House at 604.
- A small office building replaced the Dixon House at 624.

If one surveys North Green Street from its prime in the 1940s and early 1950s, one can find the original North Green Street running in front of the old first Methodist church. On both sides of North Green Street, at least twenty-five beautiful homes are gone forever.

On a personal note, Papa Harrison Taylor Martin lived on Brenau Avenue. He died before the author was born, but great-great Aunt Lutie Martin Simpson knew almost everything about our beloved Gainesville. She and Charters Smith Embry, a dear friend, filled in all of the gaps. What fun it was just remembering.

The Times Newspaper Building was constructed where the Oliver A. Carter house was located (late 1960s).

The house built at 615 Green Street was designed by Mr. Jack Bailey. It was built in the 1980s. Mr. Sandy Beaver's house was moved to the back of the lot and soon burned down.

The Hall County School Board Building and the First Baptist Church are located between Ridgewood Avenue and Holly Drive. Six houses were torn down in this location.

Hillcrest: The Home of H. H. Dean

The H. H. Dean estate was located where the First Baptist Church is on Green Street today.

The Gainesville post office was built where the W.A. Crow house stood.

The Quinlan Art Center is located at 514, on land given by Mr. Leslie Quinlan in 1955. The Gainesville Art Association was organized in 1946. The land given is diagonally across the street from where Mr. Quinlan's home was located on north Green Street.

The style is in keeping with homes on Green Street. The building is a Neoclassical Revival style and was constructed in 1964.

Quinlan Art Center

The parking lot for the Quinlan Art Center replaced the Redwine House located at 502 Green Street.

A small office building replaced the John Hulsey House located at 604 Green Street.

A small office building replaced the Dixon House located at 624 Green Street.

THE CIVIC CENTER—CIRCA 1936

Architects and Builders

Some architects and builders of houses on Green Street were found in files, reports, and interviews.

Levi Prater was born on June 15, 1872, and died on November 1, 1950. He was a self-taught builder. He built and reconstructed several houses on Green Street. Mr. Prater built the following houses on Green Street.

- Miller–Banks house in 1912.
- Adams–Smith–Edmonson–Ward house in 1925.
- Martin–Matthews–Norton house was reconstructed in 1937.
- Barrett–Whitehead house at 466 Green Street in 1930.

Mr. Evan Ledford

- Burns–Moss–Palmour-House in 1924. The house was designed by Mr. John Cherry from Atlanta.
- Miller–Banks house was renovated with the Mr. Ledford's help; the time is unknown.

Other Architects and Builders

- Mr. Patterson and Mr. Harrison designed the Jackson–Walters–Parker–Jackson house in 1909.
- Mr. John Dennis, an architect from Macon, was hired in 1951 to do extensive remodeling on the Roberts–Thurmond house.

Mr. Jack Bailey

- Designed an addition to the Martin–Matthews–Norton house in the 1970s.

- Designed the house located at 615 Green Street in the l980s.
- Designed the office building located at 604 Green Street, where Dr. John Hulsey's house was torn down.

The Hosch house was constructed in 1907 by the builders of the old First Methodist Church. Mr. John Hosch, who had the house built, was on the committee that supervised construction of the church. An interesting feature is that a prayer seat, which faced the front door, was built in the keeping and gathering room like the one at the First Methodist Church.

BIBLIOGRAPHY

Interviews and Personal Communications:

Bailey, Jack

2020   Telephone communication with Mr. Jack Bailey, Gainesville architect and designer of Green Street house plans and additions.

Hosch, Heyward C., Jr.

2020   Personal communication with Mr. Heyward C. Hosch, Jr., and tour of Hosch house property, March 6, 2020.

Norton, Frank K., Jr.

2019   Personal communication with Mr. Frank Norton about Green Street and proposed book. Received permission to use some printed materials.

Norton, Frank K. and Betty

2002   Personal communication with Mr. and Mrs. Frank Norton about business and property information on Green Street, March 3, 2020.

Sanders, Ronda, and Fouch, Michael

2020   Communication and resource materials and pictures housed at the Hall County Library, located on Academy Street in Gainesville, Georgia.

Tullar, Jessica

2019   Communication and resource materials from Jessica Tullar, AICP, Housing and Special

2020   Projects Manager, Community and Economic Development, City of Gainesville, Georgia.

Historic Resources Survey and GNAHRGIS Database

Historic Resources Survey

2019   Brockington and Associates, Inc. (O1l). Gainesville, Georgia, Community-Wide Historic Structural Survey: Prepared for the City of Gainesville Community Development Department. Atlanta: Brockington and Associates, Inc. Cultural Resources Counseling.

Survey Forms

2019   Georgia Department of Natural Resources, Historic Preservation Division, and University of Georgia's "Georgia Archaeological Site File" (2007–2011). Georgia's Natural, Archaeological, and Historic Resources GIS (GNAHRGIS).

Cloues, Richard. "House Types." New Georgia Encyclopedia. 22 August 2013. Web 1/29/2020. 2020

Sanborn Insurance Maps

Sanborn insurance maps consulted for verification of house locations and street numbers in 1909, 1915, and 1930.

Vardeman, Johnny

A resource individual from The Times newspaper who has a weekly Historical Article, and has shared a lot of information about Gainesville, Georgia. (Many years and to 2020).